Looking For a Miracle...Look Within Your Life

By a Witness, May Lewis

Looking For a Miracle...Look Within Your Life

Editor: LaBrenda Hill

Citations: Nelson, Thomas. (2007). Holy Bible (King James Version). Nashville, TN.

Copyright © 2016 by May Lewis

All rights reserved. This book or any portion thereof may not be reproduced or used in

any manner whatsoever without the express written permission of the publisher except

for the use of brief quotations in a book review or scholarly journal.

First Printing: 2017
ISBN: 978-1-365-91516-1
MAY LEWIS
Memphis, TN 38125

Dedications

This book is first dedicated to God, the Father and Jesus, His Son. It was written by me to give God the glory and the praise while in the process of feeding God's sheep. Another dedication goes out to the book of the Bible in which I meditate on day and night.

I dedicated this book to not only my grandma and mom but also to all the mothers in the world, who are exceptional human beings. I continue to give special thanks to God and to Jesus for all of them. My heart goes out to all the children of the world, who are without a doubt one of the greatest miracles given to us from God.

Of course, I cannot forget my admiring sons. I do though have to tip my hat off to one of my sons, which is a writer, as well as my reviewer. He had inspired me to be a writer instead of just chatting and blowing off hot air all the time.

Looking For a Miracle...Look Within Your Life

I would also like this book to be an encourager for all men and women whether they are young or old. I am hoping that each of my readers does decide to in some kind of a way, to help feed God's sheep, even if it is in a way that is similar to mine, becoming a writer. My love goes out to each of my readers, and may God bless us all.

Looking For a Miracle...Look Within Your Life

TABLE OF CONTENTS

FOREWORD

We often look for something spectacular to happen in our lives. If you actually take a moment and just look back deep into your own life, you can see that many things have already taken place. Yes, many miracles and signs have been evident in our own life experiences.

The very first thing that I had to do was to take a good look at my life. Once I did, what a surprise to find more miracles and signs than I could have ever imagined. We often tell ourselves, "if God did not want us to do this or that, He would actually come down and stop us or show us some type of a sign to quit what we were doing." Hold up and wait a minute, does this sound familiar?

Just go ahead and read the Bible a little closer. You would know that the Pharisees often wanted God to show miracles and signs. *"Then certain of the scribes and of the Pharisees answered, saying, Master, we would see a sign from thee" (Matthew 12:38 King James Version).* The

Looking For a Miracle...Look Within Your Life

Pharisees had always wanted to see signs and miracles from Jesus to show and prove to them if He was actually sent from God. This is still happening today, and this makes us no better off than the Pharisees were.

I am a witness that Jesus is the Son of God. My testimonies will verify that I am a believer and at the same time reveal to you the many miracles that have touched my life. God is the Truth and the only God. God is definitely still in the miracle business. By the end of this book, I assure you that your faith will have increase and you will become a true believer as I am.

Chapter 1

AT AN EARLY AGE AS A CHILD

This is the beginning of my testimony. Even as a little child, I can recall how miracles and signs repeatedly occurred in my life. *"I remember the days of old; I meditate on all thy works; I muse on the work of thy hands" (Psalm 143:5).*

When I think back to the days of my youth, I have always believed in God and knew that He was there for me. I wasn't going to let anything or anyone steal my joy or my peace. Especially, as a child, when I did not really know what was actually happening to me?

It was somewhat strange. I would often break out in a rash. This was a yearly occurrence and sometimes twice a year. It would usually last for about two weeks or more. My eyes would swell up. They would be slightly shut to an extent that they looked diagonally closed. On many occasions the outbreak would be all over my body.

Looking For a Miracle...Look Within Your Life

Yep, it ranged from my head to my toe. You name it. There were bumps in places on my body that you would have never considered. Yes, go ahead and try to visualize the part that I use to sit on.

My hands would also swell up with bumps on them. The bumps were compacted and tight. They appeared as if they would burst if you touched them. The pain was very excruciating due to the inflammation. It was very uncomfortable to use or to just lift up my hands. For example, it was hard for me to pick up a glass to drink water or for me to take my bath. When attempting to bathe myself, my mom would actually have to take over and give me a bath. As I can recall just doing my daily chores were difficult. And how often do we take doing our everyday chores for granted?

There were also bumps on other parts of my body. In addition there was a lot of itching, which caused me to do a lot of scratching. Of course, you know my nails definitely had to be cut. However, by me scratching continuously, the areas sometimes became infected. I had to wear white cotton gloves on my hands to protect me from spreading the rash onto other parts of my body. The breaking out in a rash had put me in a tough spot. It was not a pretty one. If you could only imagine how I looked. Wait, you guessed it! I would look really awful. I would think to myself, "would I ever look the same again?" I would be too embarrassed to go anywhere. I would remain inside the house during the whole episode and would not go outdoors to play. I was sorely afraid that if I came outside someone might see me and start laughing at me. To me, this was not funny and no joking matter at all!

After visiting many physicians and even going to the hospital, the doctors didn't really know what was wrong with me. They neither knew how to diagnose the illness. The doctors would all gather around and stare at me as if I was their guinea pig, waiting for the slaughter. It was embarrassing and I felt uncomfortable with each of them taking turns poking me. One of the doctors finally figured it out; that I must be allergic to something that I was eating. There was no extensive testing ever done; just mere speculation. The doctor advised my mother to keep me from eating the obvious allergic foods, such as: chocolate, seafood, and foods that had a lot of citric acid in it.

My mom was very cautious and she definitely did not want to pay more doctor bills. Therefore she speculated that other things may also be causing me allergic reactions. I was then excluded from doing most household duties in fear of me being allergic to some of the household chemicals used for cleaning the home. There were plenty of chores for us to do. Oh, what a great opportunity it was for me to be taken away from some of those chores! However, this really made my brother and sister angry because now all the chores fell in their laps and it was between the two of them to carry out the load.

Looking For a Miracle...Look Within Your Life

Each time after these rash incidents, there was a miracle brewing. Yes, an unseen wonder that no one could have ever imagined. My skin went through a transformation that was similar to a snake shedding from old skin to new skin. I had the most beautiful skin that you could have ever seen or thought to imagine. My skin became so soft to the touch. It felt like a soft pillow or cuddly teddy bear. Even today, I occasionally get compliments on how soft my skin is.

Although my skin became more beautiful and softer, there was always a reminder left behind. A mark was clearly left visible on my body to remind me about each outbreak. No, it was not a big mark, but the size was large enough for me to know that it was there now, and it was not there before my outbreak had taken place. I knew that only God could have brought me through these rugged situations. The rash was only a small price to pay for an outcome that brought me such soft and beautiful skin. The whole experience of me breaking out in that rash often goes

through my mind and reminds me of how great God was

back then at my early age; and without a doubt He still is

now.

Chapter 2

TRAVELING MERCY

Another miracle happened while I was traveling on vacation with my family. We had often driven from California to Mississippi, which is our home state. It was roughly a 36-hours drive. Yes, you may say that we were sort of homesick. We also knew deep in our hearts that our family would not be dropping in on us in California. Therefore, we had to drive back and forth to see them. Bear in mind, the plane fare was expensive too. Therefore, it was most cost-effective for us to drive being a family of four.

As always when traveling, we would often drive until we got tired and then we would switch drivers. On this particular trip, I had been driving for a while. It was time to switch places with my ex-spouse. When I looked over at him, he was sound asleep. Being considerate, I thought to myself that I would drive a little while longer in order for him to get plenty rest. I drove for a bit and then fell asleep at the wheel. While I was asleep, I noticed that there was somebody up in the sky. His hair was dark black. He was wearing a white robe. Yes, it was p-h-e-n-o-m-e-n-a-l! Jesus was His name. I guess by now you are asking yourself how I knew it was Jesus. Let me share this little bit of information with you. The reason I knew that it was Jesus was because of all the illustrations I had seen before of Jesus. In comparison, they looked identical.

Jesus had the palm of His hands stretched out towards me, as if, He was giving me permission to come. Suddenly, I woke up and drove to the next rest stop. I was scared and amazed all at the same time. While at the rest area, I went to the bathroom. While walking to the restroom as well as while using the bathroom I began contemplating on what had just happened. Afterwards, I got back in the car and drove yet some more. I guess you can say that I was wide awake then. I drove for about two more hours and then switched places with my ex-spouse.

At the time of the occurrence, I did not mention this to my family. It was mostly due to not wanting to scare or to wake them. I was flabbergasted. I knew that this was breathtaking. This was real and definitely, a serious matter. However, I kept thinking about what did God wanted me to do. I knew that I should have switched places and let my ex-spouse drive awhile. In addition, I realized that God was not finished with me yet or with my family. Jesus had compassion on us. It was a miracle that my family and I were not all dead. There was not one scratch on us or on the car.

Later on, I finally told my family what had happened while I was driving to our family's home in Mississippi. Next, I told the church congregation what had happened on our trip. Of course, now I tell quite a few people. It appears that the deeper my relationship got with

Looking For a Miracle...Look Within Your Life

God, I would inform more and more people about what had happened. I wanted everyone to know just how great God is.

I can see now, without a doubt, that God definitely has a plan for me. *"For the Lord of host hath purposed, and who shall disannul it? and his hand is stretched out, and who shall turn it back" (Isaiah 14:27)?* I realized that God had more work for me to do here on earth. Even with me mistakenly falling asleep while driving certainly could not interfere with His plan. I have seen the glory of God. This experience alone is enough reason why I give praises daily to God and Jesus. I believe that we all have encountered some type of close-to-death event in our lives. We just have not fully marinated on it yet. While I was traveling from California, I had one of my own. Thank God for His mercy. He keeps giving us that "one more chance" that we repeatedly ask for, and of course, we still do nothing with it.

Chapter 3

MY BELOVED GRANDMA

Some miracles are those that might not have happened directly to us, but still had a tremendous impact on our lives. My grandma played an important role in this type of situation. Even though the miracle had happened long before my time, it definitely had a positive effect on my life. My grandma was a one-in-a-billion kind of person.

This miracle happened when my mother was a child. My mom told me that my grandma was extremely sick. Mom stated that since it was during the time she was very young, the experience is somewhat vague in her memory exactly all of grandma's symptoms. She knew that is was a very sad memory. Grandma's vital signs were abnormal. She had lost enormous weight. Neither my family nor the doctors knew exactly what was wrong with her.

Looking For a Miracle…Look Within Your Life

My grandma eventually had to be hospitalized. While she stayed in the hospital no one would clean up her room, except for this one particular person. Other housecleaning workers would not go into her room. Their rationale may have been that she may have been contagious, not going to be around too long, or maybe something similar to those magnitudes. The doctors tried all types of procedures to heal her but without success. In their minds, there was nothing else left for them to try to do for her to make her well. The doctors at the hospital had given up on my grandma. They also stated that she would not make it; no hope for her to live. She will be dead within a few months. Therefore, the doctors decided to send my grandma home. They stated that it would be better and more fulfilling for her to have her last few months at home with her family.

My granddad took my grandma home knowing that it was nothing he could do to make her better. My mother stated that he later decided to pack up and leave town with the family. They all moved to the countryside. On the next day after leaving town, a great miracle happened. My grandma was actually able to get up out of the bed. It was remarkable! It appeared that all her illness was gone. She started feeling better. Within weeks, she was able to gain all her weight back. My grandma was able to get back to her old habits. She had started doing her daily tasks around the house. She was feeling fabulous.

I am so glad that my grandma overcame that tribulation because my grandma had been a great inspiration to me. I can say that I had two mommas. My grandma was a true believer in God. *"Jesus answered and said unto them, This is the work of God, that ye believe on him whom he had sent" (John 6:29)*. My grandma definitely believed that Jesus was sent by God. She made sure that she instilled that into us.

Looking For a Miracle...Look Within Your Life

One of the ways she exhibited that behavior was when we were about to eat lunch while sitting around the dining table. My grandma asked my sister to say the grace. My sister started hesitating before saying the grace. She stated that she would be saying the grace that she knew which began with "God is grace." I remembered grandma telling us at that time; "If you do not know what to say, just say two words, 'Jesus wept'" That would be sufficient to show God how thankful you are for the food that He has provided.

My grandma definitely had the fear of God in her. You could always tell by her actions that she always put God first in her life. For instance, if there was any type of inclement weather outside, lighting or thundering, she would tell us to turn off the television while God does His work. She also told us to sit down and be quite. I guess she believed that God must have been angry at the world or maybe just us. At least this is what I thought at first. Then, later on, I found out that it was much deeper than that. When my grandma was a little girl, her mother had been struck by lightning and died. At the time, her mother was cutting wood. Of course, she did not want this type of incident to happen to us. She knew by firsthand why you should be still when God is doing His mighty works.

Another thing about my grandma is that she did not have much, but she would give you the shirt off her back. She would help any one of her family members or friends. She was very unselfish. If anyone of them needed a place to stay, she would let them stay awhile with us until he or she were able to get back on his or her feet. At the time, I was young and did not really understand. It was mainly due to knowing that we did not have much for us to sustain ourselves and could not really afford another person to stay with us.

I can now testify that I was able to see my grandma. If this miracle of healing her and extending my grandma's life span had not happened, I would have never had a chance to meet her. And as you recall when this entire miracle took place it was before I was born. My grandma lived to be 99 years young. I thank God for this miracle, which showed me how great God's work is if you keep your faith in Him and put Him first. This was truly a blessing shown to my family and especially to me. This miracle allowed my grandma to live as long as she did in order for her to hand down her traits to us and many other generations.

Chapter 4

MIDDLE SCHOOL AGE LESSON

I thank God for His grace and mercy on me even when I have done wrong. His light continues to shine on me. I was told by my mom; "If you do right, right will follow you. If you do not, it will not." This statement had always made a long lasting impression on me.

I had always believed in God. Therefore, I tried to obey His Commandments from the time that I can remember. Although as a youth, around middle school age, I did something mischievous. I had strayed away from doing what is right. I had asked mom earlier that day if I could ride my bike. I had wanted to ride so bad that it left an unpleasant taste in my mouth.

My mother had told me specifically not to my ride my bike. Of course, you know what she stated went into one ear and went out the other ear. I was disappointed, but in my mind determined that I was going to ride my bike today regardless of what she had said. That opportunity had come in a flash. Yes, it was knocking loud on my door. My mother had to go to the store. I knew that this was my moment to do what I had wanted to do all morning. As soon as, I saw the car going down the street with my mother. I went directly into the back bedroom and got my bike.

I started riding my bike. I knew that I would not be caught because I knew how long it took mom to shop for grocery. If you think about it too, for only a quick second, you should be able to relate as well, how long our moms take to shop for grocery. It was as if they were having a night out in the town and wanted to see everything. I knew that my mom would be going down every aisle in the store. It was going to take at least two hours or more before she would be finished.

While riding my bike, I was having the best fun of my life. I had been going up and down the streets and around the blocks. The time was flying by. Then suddenly I realized that it was about time for mother to come home. I had to make certain that I was back at home and my bike put up as if I had never ridden it. Therefore, I decided one last trip to put my sister on the back of the bike and ride home. Once we turned the corner, my bike front wheel went one way and my sister and I went another. We got up and made certain we were both okay. There was not a scratch on my sister. As for me, I had scrubbed my finger badly on the concrete. I could see the white part under my skin. I knew right then that I was being paid back for being disobedient.

"Children, obey your parents in the Lord, for this is right" (Ephesians 6:1). I did not obey my mom. I did not do what was right. I remembered what my mom had always told me and that kept going through my mind; "if you do right and right will follow you." I prayed to God please do not let me get a whipping. I knew I deserved it. I

was wrong, but I knew in my mind that this whipping was really going to be a "beat down." It was going to be the worst whipping that I had ever had in my life.

I had to tell mom what I had done. The funniest thing is that she would have known anyway. Due to my injury she would have proof that I was disobedient. I could not hide my finger. I started looking at my finger again and again and the more I looked the more frantically I prayed. If you knew my mom then you would know that she did not play. I definitely did know her. Believe me when I say that I never had to get a whipping for the same thing twice. My finger continued to hurt badly and now I knew my gluteus maximus would be too. This was going to be an awful combination.

Mom finally came back from the store. I told her what had happened and she looked at my finger thoroughly and then looked at me and said that I have already been punished enough. What a big surprise to me. I did not get a whipping. God had answered my prayers. I had never ever recalled being that defiant before. I knew at that moment that it was a sign from God for me to behave and to be obedient to my mom. It was definitely a mind-blowing miracle to me that I did not get a whipping, when I had directly disobeyed her instructions. God is great! As a matter of fact, God is f-a-n-t-a-s-t-i-c!

Now do not think for a moment that I did not have to answer for being disobedient. God did so in His own way. I was in dreadful burning pain for weeks with my finger and it seems like it took forever for my finger to be completely healed. I can still see the long mark that was left on my finger from this incident. In addition, I could not ride my bike for a very long time because my front wheel needed to be repaired. Of course, you already know that my mom was not in a hurry to get it fixed. I knew that this was a great lesson that I was being taught and a well-deserved one. As mom always said "when you do not do what is right then how do you expect right to follow you."

Chapter 5

HOLIDAY WONDERS

Through meditation, I am often reminded how Jesus was able to feed so many with only a small amount of food. As an adult, I had doubted in a similar situation when trying to feed just only a few. This occurrence happened to me on one Christmas Day.

I prayed that our holiday would not be ruined due to not having enough food to feed ourselves, as well as an additional member of the family that had sneaked upon us spontaneously. Throughout the whole time, I was thinking to myself, I hope that she did not want anything to eat, but I knew that was just wishful thinking.

Everyone knows that during the holiday season everybody wants something to eat even though it was not bought or cooked by him or her. God has always ensured in the past we had enough to eat, but since it was during the holidays it made me start second-guessing. *"Do ye not yet understand, neither remember the five loaves of the five thousand, and how many baskets ye took up" (Matthew 16:9)?* This verse became a reality to me. I prayed to God and made a petition that was parallel to this verse. While I was asking God, I then started reminiscing on similar times on what He had done beforehand and was wondering if He would provide us with enough food again.

As part of one of the menu items for the day, I had cooked some greens. The greens had withered up. After shrinking, it was not enough to feed us and definitely not an additional person. Nevertheless, this particular relative had been extra kind to us. How could we turn her away? Of course, we absolutely did not want to turn her away regardless of our situation. I was thinking to myself; "what in the world are we going to do?" I started contemplating that maybe I needed to try to go out and get something else to eat. In regards to money, I knew that our money was short. All the thanks goes to God. It turned out that day that I was not only able to feed the relative that showed up but it was a plenty enough greens and food for the family and I to eat and enjoy. There was also food left over for the next day.

Did I forget to mention that all the food was delicious too? Of course, it was with God's help. I thanked God once again for us having ample food on this Christmas Day. In addition, that was the best tasting greens that I had in a long time. You may think to yourself that this does not sound like a miracle. You have to have been there and seen how small the amounts of greens were. Let me explain it a little better. If you had ever cooked or witnessed someone cooking greens and seen the greens at the beginning to end, you would know how they wither up. If you have not, just imagine washing lettuce with hot water and seeing how small it gets. You would have to rethink and say that it must have been truly amazing for me to have enough greens for everyone.

The relative enjoyed it so much that she asked if she could come back next Christmas. Of course, you know what my first thought was; "Oh no." I had to remember once again that God got us through this one and He would get us through the next one. I stated to her that she can surely come back and we would enjoy her company. God is always there when you need a helping hand even when you think you do not need Him.

Is not God still doing spectacular things in our lives? Even when we are not conscious of what is happening. No, I did not feed thousands of individuals on that day, but I did have enough food for us all and some left over for the next day. That, in itself, was truly a blessing.

You do not have to feed thousands to believe. I have faith in God and thank God for even the so-called "small miracles." We have to stop being so doubtful and believe!

Chapter 6

MEDITATING ON BIBLE VERSES

A good example of how you can tell if I am a true believer of God and His miracles is by the way I fashion my day. My daily routine starts out by giving God the praises and it ends the same by giving God the praises. One example is one day while meditating; it was as though I was able to understand a certain chapter in the Bible really well.

Even though I had read this chapter many times before in the past and even memorized it, after reading Psalm 23 again, it was astounding that I could comprehend it with no problem. I will reveal to you shortly what was placed on my mind regarding the six verses in this chapter. Some individuals can ordinarily pick up a magazine or book regarding different types of subject matter and read it in its entirety. Yet, if you would ask some of those same individuals, they will tell you that they have not read the entire Bible at least once. On the contrary, I would pick up a Bible and read anywhere from one to four chapters or more throughout the day. In addition, not only do I read at home but also one of the first things that I do when I get to work is pick up a Bible. Yes, this may be just the opposite of what you or others might do. Certainly, I do read other books but only when it is necessary. I put reading God's Word first at the top of my list.

Let me now divulge to you what was entered through my mind that day when I was meditating on Psalm 23. The meaning of the verses from this specific chapter as I mentioned previously was as clear as daylight. I distinctly noted the verse first and the meaning thereafter in parenthesis. All of these verses, which I will be relating to had all come from the King James Version of the Holy Bible. I would start with the very first verse and then gradually work my way through the end of the chapter. This is what transpired, as I was reading Psalm 23... *"The*

Lord is my shepherd" (Master, my God and no other gods before me); *I shall not want* (God has everything, no need to ask for nothing).

While I was contemplating further on the verses, I thought if I do what is right according to God's eyes and pursue after God's Kingdom first, He will give me everything that I need and it does not always mean it will be everything that I want. This concept is also the next to the last thing that I say in my daily prayers before I conclude with "in Jesus' name we pray."

Continuing with the second verse of Psalm 23..."*He maketh me to lie down in green pastures* (good land, shelter, place to stay, rest, and house): *he leadeth me beside the still waters"* (peace). Thirdly, relating to the next stanza..."*He restoreth my soul* (forgive my sins): *he leadeth me in the paths of righteousness for his name's sake"* (not right by our eyes, but by the image of God).

The fourth verse says:...."*Yea, though I walk through the valley of the shadow of death*" (a lot of killing, dying around me), "*I will fear no evil* (faith)*: for thou art with me; thy rod and thy staff they comfort me*" (protection round about; hands around me).

Next the fifth section..."*Thou preparest a table before me in the presence of mine enemies*" (give me food; give me victory): "*thou anointest my head with oil*" (rebuke the demons/haters); "m*y cup runneth over*" (have many miracles; blessings).

Finally the sixth verse...."*Surely goodness and mercy shall follow me all the days of my life*" (do right, right will follow you always): "a*nd I will dwell in the house of the Lord for ever*" (in church continuously, not with evil doers).

This particular chapter in Psalm and its meanings that I have just witnessed to you was as transparent as spring water to me. The words were gushing out and this is

Looking For a Miracle...Look Within Your Life

why I decided to share them with you. Remember that God will provide your needs, guide you in the right direction, and protect you from all harm and danger.

I am hoping that my clarification of the verses in Psalm 23 carry you through some good and hard times as it has done for me. Another desire that I have is for God to continue to bless your soul. Alongside, you heeding closely to follow God's Words while meditating on Bible verses to get a clearer understanding from God.

Chapter 7

POST-DELIVERY GRACE

The doctors were trying to make me have my baby naturally. They tried and tried. After pushing and pushing, for such a long time, I was still in labor for almost 24 hours with no prevail of having it naturally. Since I had failed to have it naturally, I had to get a C-section.

The birth of my baby had come at a great cost. The price was that I had endured was a lot of pain, in which, in return made me rethink long and hard if I ever wanted to have a child again. The miracle that I will emphasize was during my post-delivery time.

Following the delivery of my baby and after coming from surgery, this miracle happened. A nurse was showing special attention to me more than the other nurses were. The nurse was also a nun in which she wore a habit outfit. She was very nice to me and made sure that I was okay. She kept coming back and forth to ensure I had everything

I needed. She was very concerned. She kept checking my vitals, especially my temperature and blood pressure.

At that particular point in time, I was a very young adult. Let me just tell you a little secret. I definitely was not an angel. I was having a baby out of wedlock. Yes, God still cares for us even when we have been mischievous. God loves all of us in spite of our faults. Sometimes we, as people, forget that having a baby is a blessing from God. We treat it as a bad thing almost as if it was a curse. Undeniably, we tend to follow sinful practices...unplanned pregnancy. Nevertheless, it does not change the fact that children are still one of the greatest miracles given to us from God. Keeping this in mind, we are the ones that make mistakes, not God.

All during my post-delivery time, I was shaking furiously. Doctors did not know why, but of course, God definitely knew. My first thought was that the shaking could have been from me being so afraid right before delivering my baby. The nun nurse repeatedly stated to me to try to stop shaking. As if I had real control of what was happening. She explained that if I do not stop shaking soon it may indicate something else could seriously be wrong with me. However, it could be something as simple as the cold IV fluids that were put in my body, my hormone changing, or the effect of the anesthesia or the endorphin.

I was hoping that everything would be okay. I was also wishing that nothing serious would have to be done to me to make me stop shaking. I just kept on believing and praying that I would be okay and I would stop shaking. Then again, I knew I would be okay because I knew that God was still in control. I was asking for His help even though I did not deserve it. Especially knowing why I was in this position in the first place. After a long while I finally stopped shaking. The nun nurse *(by the look on her face)* seemed more relieved than me that I had stopped shaking. I knew that God had performed his wonders on me.

Early the next day I had spoken to one of the nurses and told her how wonderful the nun nurse was. I gave her the description of the nun nurse that was working that night. I also mentioned to her that the nun nurse's demeanor was awesome and it was the best I had witnessed. She looked at me and said that there is no one of that description that worked or volunteered here, not on the day or on the night shift. I asked others that worked at the hospital and they also confirmed that there was not a nun nurse, with that description that worked at the hospital. I knew then at that moment God must have sent a guardian angel to look after me during my post-delivery time. *"For he shall give his angels charge over thee, to keep thee in all thy ways" (Psalms 91:11).* It was good to know that regardless of my mischievous ways that God had still sent an angel to take care of me while I was in the hospital. It was phenomenal. This was such a great wonder to me.

During my whole stay, which was a couple of weeks in the hospital, I had never seen that individual again. I guess you could say that her deed was done.

Chapter 8

GUIDANCE AFTER DIVORCE

We often go through some things in our lifetime that makes us wonder did we make the right decision. It has us sometimes questioning ourselves. For me, one of my uncertainties was about my divorce. Particularly, when I knew that getting a divorce was an important matter in God's eyes. Therefore, I had to remember to keep my trust in God. This special miracle happened to me right after my divorce.

I was rationalizing to myself, if it is truly meant to be, God would have made it happen. I knew that God had a plan. *"And we know that all things work together for good to them that love God, to them who are the called according to his purpose" (Romans 8:28).* I had to remember that God had already worked this out for me. I had to keep my faith and know that it would be beneficial. At the moment, I was not able to see it clearly. However, I knew that I would be able to perceive it very soon. The reason for my divorce would materialize at the appropriate time.

This encounter happened while I was unaccompanied at home in Georgia. At the time, I was praying to God. I was being submissive. I guess you can say that I was really questioning God. I was asking Him about my marriage. Why was the divorce happening to me? While I was talking, I was crying. There were many tears being cried or can I say rivers of tears. I kept asking God, "why?" "What did I do?" What did I do to deserve this to be happening to me? I knew that I had been faithful in my marriage and that is why I kept rationalizing.

At this particular time, I was the only one in the room as well as in the house. I heard a deep voice plainly state: "that it is not about you." I knew that something p-h-e-n-o-m-e-n-a-l had just happened. I believed that God had spoken to me. I did not ask God for an explanation. I started thinking and thought that it must have been all about my ex-spouse. Afterward, I was not feeling guilty about being divorce. The guilt I felt came from me wondering if I had let God down by leaving. After I accepted I did not, then I felt at peace about my divorce.

Previously in the past I had always prayed for God to keep my marriage, just as others do. As I got a closer bond with God, I started saying, "let Your will be done." However when you say this, you have to be ready for whatever comes your way. It may not be what "you" had desire. You have to remember that it is God's plan you are requesting to happen. His plan may not be what you actually have envisioned. I knew, deep inside, that everything that will occur would work out for my good. Who else knows me better than anyone else or even myself...only God does. Many things started transforming after I accepted God's will. It was all for the better. I gave in to God and let Him start taking over my steering wheel.

Looking For a Miracle...Look Within Your Life

My life began to turn around. God had made many changes in my life. One of them was allowing all of my bills to be consolidated. The bills were now better to grip and easier to pay.

I moved out of our five bedrooms, five baths house with a basement in Georgia to distant myself from any conflict that may had risen from our divorce. Nevertheless, I was not in despair. I knew that God would be providing me with a place to stay more fitting for His cause. I relocated to a city in my home state of Mississippi. I was now much closer to my grandma and mom. I could now leave at the drop of a hat. I was able to visit and it was less than a three-hours drive. It reminded me of a weekend get-a-way rather than a planned vacation. God was working it all out for me. I later went back to school and finished my bachelor degree. I was now doing things that I had put aside on the back burner when I was married.

Yet, after all these things had happened, I still did not have it all together as to what God actually meant for me after my divorce. Later on, I finally realized that it was not about my ex-spouse. This was not learned until I had reached another level in my relationship with God. I started doing more sacrificing, following God's law, and began giving more of my time to God. My whole attitude changed. I was not the same.

I knew now what obtaining my divorce meant when God had stated, "that it was not about me." I realized that God meant it was all about Him. Yes, it was about the One and Only true God and it was never about my ex-spouse nor about me. I was finally thinking clearer. I had taken off the blindfolds. What God had really wanted me to do was to give Him the glory, honor, the praise, and of course, also my heart.

Chapter 9

AIRBORNE FAVOR

This particular miracle happened within months of finishing this book. I was thinking not to include this miracle since the table of contents had already been established. I do have to admit though that God's miracles do not stop just because I am writing a book. God showed favor on me while I was airborne on a flight from Chicago.

I was on my way to catch the connecting flight. While I was rushing through the airport to catch the train to my gate of departure, there was a woman standing in middle of the aisle. She stated that she was sorry that I had missed my plane. Huh...Huh! What was this woman implying?

The matter of fact was I had not missed my plane. Besides, if it were so, how would she have known? This woman continued talking and asked me how much did I pay for my ticket. I stated to her that this was a business trip. I continued walking. She stated for me to wait. I told her that I had to go and I continued stepping before I actually do miss my plane.

I proceeded to the gate. I started boarding the plane along with the other passengers. We were finally in flight. After we had been flying in the air for about 30 minutes, I observed that the stewards had not yet handed out the snacks and our flight was only for one hour twenty minutes. Normally by now, they would have begun passing out the refreshments. I began second-guessing and thinking that maybe we are not going to get any snacks. Then my ears started hurting. As always, I started going through the motion of acting as if I was chewing gum. This technique had always helped me out in the past. The pain start getting worse and worse. The woman sitting next to me started looking at me. We began staring at each other while picking at our ears. I knew that something was just not right. All of sudden, the aisle was full of smoke. The smoke was foggy white. It appeared as if someone had widely opened a freezer door. The temperature on the plane became hot. It was getting hotter and hotter by the minute. I started wondering. "What is truly happening?" I began praying. Everyone on the plane started looking at each other. We knew that something strange was going on. None of the crewmembers came on the intercom to explain what was happening. A man passenger in front of me hit the call button. This man had the appearance of a pilot, because he wore what resembled a pilot outfit.

After a while, one of the stewards came down the aisle and started speaking to the man. I was gazing at the steward along with trying to overhear their conversation. I then looked directly into the steward's eyes. He had much fear in his eyes. About that same time our pilot came on the intercom and explained that we had lost cabin pressure. He stated that he had to lower the plane's altitude. He mentioned that we should be landing soon, but to the same airport we had just left. I said to myself that he must have mistakenly uttered the incorrect airport. He then stated due to what he had seen displayed on the plane's navigation screen that he had to turn the plane around. In addition, he mentioned that he was sorry about how hot it was. Due to the problems we encountered, the air conditioner had to be turn off.

A little while later the pilot landed the plane. I understood at that moment a miracle had just happened and God had shown favor on us. I knew that Jesus must have put His arms around the plane and that was the reason why we had landed safely. I am glad I kept my faith in God. It does not cost anything to have faith, but it is priceless. *"For by grace are ye saved through faith; and that not of yourselves: it is the gift of God: Not of works, lest any man should boast" (Ephesians 2:8-9).* Grace was not set at a fee for us. God wanted us to know that it was not given to us based on how much we could afford, according to what we deserve, or what we have done. The unrestricted grace was given because of God's love for us.

Despite of all the things that we have done in our lives and are still doing, we do not deserve the favor that God keeps giving us. It was great to know that God was the true pilot that day and had everything in control. If you had only just seen our faces, you would have known how thankful we were for God's mercy. We were later told by the area manager that the former crew did not want to fly another flight. I knew then that it must have been extremely bad if the pilot did not want to fly another plane. Neither did any of the crewmembers wanted to get on another plane. The area manager stated that, they would be getting all new crewmembers and if there are any questions we could come to the information desk to get an explanation of the whole situation.

I started wondering even more why an explanation of what had just happened was not put on the intercom for every one of us to hear. If not, we should have been asked to approach the desk as a group instead of individually. At the same time, they were all being very generous. The representatives of the airline were really trying hard to accommodate us. They offered us different kinds of snacks as well as ice that was conveniently ready for us. We were able to serve ourselves and there were no constraints placed on obtaining as many items as you like.

I had always been told by my mom that God never slips anything up on you. He always gives you some type of forewarning. We just have to take notice of what is directly in front of us. We have to open up our eyes. When I reflect about that day I remembered the woman that stated that I had missed my plane. She was being very persistent. I believe this woman was sent by God to try to tell me something. I believe that I was not supposed to have been on that flight just as the woman had insinuated earlier when she told me that I had missed my plane. However, since I was not detained and continued on to the gate and had

gotten on the plane God showed mercy and protected me

on the flight. The clues were definitely there. I was not

paying attention not being in a hurry to listen or to take

notice of the signs. I thank God for His favor that He had

shown, not only to me that day while flying, but also to all

of us that was on the plane.

Chapter 10

MY DARLING MOM

Another miracle that I have to mention before I end this book occurred during the era when my mother was a child. Before I reveal this miracle to you let me tell you a little something first about my mom. My mother was a type of person that will give you her last. During my childhood she was the nicest mom that I knew. She had the biggest heart even though she was quite firm with her discipline.

Let me just go ahead and key in right there for a second regarding her big heart. I can recall an instance relating to a piece of chicken. My mom had finished cooking and we had sat down to eat dinner. After I had eaten my portion, I asked mom for another piece of chicken. I asked mainly out of greed, and of course, I would have to acknowledge that the chicken was delicious.

Looking For a Miracle...Look Within Your Life

Even though it was the last piece of chicken and she had not eaten her share yet; she said, "Yes" without hesitating.

My mom had always been a type of person willing to give you her last and her all. Yes, this type of agape love is what God wants us to have for each other. *"This is my commandment, that ye love one another, as I have loved you" (John 15:12).* God showed His love for us by allowing His Son to die for our sins. Now that is definitely love.

I have to confess that I experienced the same situation with my kids when they were growing up as my mom had with me. They had asked for the last piece of chicken when they had already eaten their portion. I thought to myself, at least let me just taste the chicken. Therefore, my immediate response to my kids was that I would give you half of it. I knew my kids were only thinking of themselves. I have to admit, I was thinking more of myself as well. I was willing to budge, but not as much as my mother had done with me when I was younger. In a way, that is a perfect example of how families, with each generation, become a little more selfish. This occurs without anyone even noticing it.

Mom believed in God. She made sure my siblings and I went to church each Sunday morning not only attending the worship service, but also Sunday school. Even on the days when she could not go due to other commitments she made sure we attended. Another quick attribute about my mom was that she was a very quiet person. She was the type of person that did not verbally express that she loved you, but would show it to you in her actions. I was younger then and did not pay much attention to what was said or not said. Even though I knew without a doubt that love was in the atmosphere.

Now that I look back and remember the word "love" it was used sporadically. It is different now. In these days we get to hear "I love you" a lot, but folks' action shows you just the opposite of it. The word is actually losing its value because we are forgetting the true meaning of love, which should be demonstrated in our actions and not just in our lip-syncing. It is best for someone not to say the word love if they do not actually mean it. It does more damage to a person when someone says it and his or her action does not reflect the meaning of love but shows something entirely different. I would rather for someone to "show" me that he or she loves me. The action of caring they would display will definitely be unforgettable.

Enough have been expressed concerning my mom's personality. Now let me go ahead and tell you about the miracle. This miracle took place on a c-o-l-d day. Back in those days the stove and heater were made in such a way that you could actually see the fire in it. Mom stated it was customary for you to stand close to the stove or heater to get warmer. In addition, she stated it was normal for you to be positioned with your back toward the heat whether you were by a stove or by a heater. One particular day, my mother was trying to keep warm and was standing by the stove. After standing there for a while, the back of her dress caught on fire. My mother told me that she started panicking. Her first instinct was for her to run outdoors. She ran suddenly to the door. She stated that after opening the front door she then tried to open the screen door, but she could not. The latch on the screen door was in a locked position. Since my mom was a short woman in stature, the latch was too high up on the screen door for her to reach it.

During this time her brother was playing in the living room. Her sister was also nearby washing clothes in the kitchen. Her sister noticed that my mom's dress was on fire and quickly threw the wash water on her back. My aunt's quick reaction helped save my mom's life. As a result of the burn and the water being thrown on her back, her back had blistered. She was burned from her back to the top of her gluteus maximus. It was hard for her to attempt to sit down. It was a very unpleasant time for my mom. The pain was unbearable. The doctor had to put a wooden bottle crate with an electrical light bulb on her back to help dry up the skin. She had to lie on her stomach continuously. She was only allowed to get up to eat and to use the restroom.

The lying on her stomach technique for her burned wounds to heal took six months before it actually cleared up. My mom mentioned that nowadays they would have probably drafted skin from other parts of her body to help the progression of recovery. My mom stated that she is grateful to be alive. She stated that if the screen door had not been locked she would have went outside and the fire would have devoured her. This is why I can say, without a doubt, if it had not been for God's mercy mom would not be alive today and neither would I, as far as that matters. God had done this miracle of saving my mom from the flames. I am witness to the scars on her back where she was severely burned. Her back has been totally healed. This is another reason why I believe and continue to give God the praise.

Chapter 11

L-O-V-E IS THE SOLUTION

Although I am a believer, I still struggle at times with putting God first in my life. Sometimes according to the environment that I am in, it appears that I leave God at the door; as if He actual needs permission or if he does not meet the security check to come in. Therefore, sometimes I have to thump myself on the head to get back to reality.

I also have to admit that my attitude sometimes may be unlovable in some ways. And this should not be. I should be the same no matter where I am. My heart should always be in the right place including God in whatever I do, and to be an example for others.

The problems we face in this world comes from numerous sources. Nevertheless, I feel that the main source is selfishness. We think more about pleasing ourselves rather than others. For example I can recall while writing a paper for college I was trying to figure out the solution to the problems that we were facing in this world. Suddenly, something came over me. It was the answer to the solution, and it was as clear as day. I believe the best way to resolve these problems is as simple as a four-letter word. That word is "l-o-v-e," which in essence God is love. We need to start loving one another as God loves us.

God wants us to have unconditional love. The kind of love for one another in spite of what he or she has done. L-o-v-e is the most valuable component that is missing in our lives today. Love is not only the solution to the problems that we encounter but, also the answer to having true success. It is important that we understand that God is the source of love. Loving one another is part of knowing our Father, who is God. We all say that we love and believe in God. If we truly do, it would show in our actions throughout the week, and not just on Sunday morning when the preacher says to give each other a "high-five" clap.

Looking For a Miracle...Look Within Your Life

Love is so important and powerful, even weighted above faith and hope. This is why it is imperative to love one another. It is not what some people might think; that sex is love, but love is much deeper. Love is what comes from your heart. Sex is only a part of a way to exhibit love, but it is not "all" love. Some individuals may think salvation is the solution to all of our problems that we face in this world. *"And by him all that believe are justified from all things, from which ye could not be justified by the law of Moses" (Act 13:39).* Salvation is the justification. Even though salvation plays a big part in the solution. Salvation, however, is only part of the answer. Just to reiterate, salvation is the justification, but love is the solution. It all begins with God's love. Due to God's love for us, He allowed His son Jesus Christ to die on the cross for our sins. Now is that not a good example of what you call true love? How many individuals can truly say that they would do that? You can probably count them on one hand, or maybe one finger.

Another thing that we have to do is to be fair to everyone. We need to treat everybody with love and kindness. We should be more like a tight-knit family to each other and show love to all, and not just to the ones in our clique. Everyone should be united as one. Whether you want to consider it or not, God is the answer to our every day-to-day operation. His love is endless. L-o-v-e is a contagious condition. When utilized, it spreads, and the next individual that catches it scatters the love to others.

Once you allow love into your heart you will realize that it was the missing remedy needed in order to have true success. True success in our lives entails our love, health and our soul. Love allows you to be at peace and be able to see the meaningfulness in your life more clearly. Keep in mind, we may suffer sometimes in life, just as Jesus went through some pain while here on earth; the problems we endure will make us better equipped to help others and to comfort them through their trials and tribulations. Life is really all about encouraging one another to help make each other better.

Thanks, through the grace of God we have salvation. God made us all. We are in His image so just tell me why is it that sometimes we act differently when we are away from church? We behave unlovable to others. Here is a news flash; "God is everywhere." We need to show love to everyone at all times. Yes, even to the ones that are on our jobs and ones that are at the ball games. We have to remember that the master key to everything, as well as the solution, is love. God is love. Now, go out and try this solution, and you will find out that in all circumstances that it does work. Better yet, I know that once you have tried it, you definitely will love it.

Chapter 12

RECOGNIZING YOUR MIRACLES

These are just some of my testimonies that I have witnessed to you. Yes, there were many more wonders and signs that I could have mentioned. However these stuck out like a sore thumb. God often substantiates His existence by showing us signs and miracles.

My testimonies were to give you just a taste of what God has done for me. By sharing my testimonies I hope that you can also recognize the miracles that have happened in your life. Then you will see without a doubt all God has done for you, and you will become a believer if you are not already.

The miracles in your life could have been big or small. Whether your miracles are not as significant as you might think or hope they would be. It could be similar to Jesus turning water into wine, or perhaps not getting a whipping by your parent when you were truly defiant. On the other hand, the miracles may have been as crucial as the one with my grandmother when doctors had told you that you were not going to make it, and later on you survive and live as my grandmother *(99 years young)*. Nevertheless, by now you should have gotten the picture. God is still in control, showing up at the right time, and unmovable in running His establishment.

All of the wonders that you have just read should be transparent to you if you just think about the different things that have happened to you in your life. You should not have to think too long or too hard. I believe you can also recall many miracles and signs. *"Then said Jesus unto him, Except ye see signs and wonders, ye will not believe"* *(John 4:48)*. After reading about all these wonders and signs are you still faithless and saying that you have not had any miracles or signs in your life? If so, you may want to take time out and read this book again. I hope by rereading it you would then believe, and with certainty be able to confess to others.

My love for God had me wanting to find some kind of a way to help feed God's sheep, and I chose writing. I thought about it deeply and said to myself that God is still doing today what He has done in the past. He is still preforming miracles. This is specifically what is mentioned in the Bible. We are just not currently recording the miracles and feeling the importance of them as we have done historically. Yet, they are all still real.

I wrote this book so it could be used as another way to feed God's flock. I am presenting another spin on things in order to do His will. By doing His will I will not give into my own selfish wants. I have faith that God would give me all that I needed to make this book happen. Perhaps you may be thinking right now at this moment that I do not have it all "down pat." You may be right.

However, I do know that with God's help He will guide me and lead me in the right direction.

If I can get you now to be a little bit more serious. I need you to start writing down all that God has brought you through. You should then be able to see clearly how God have done many miracles in your life. If not, think about a time in your life when you may not have had anything to eat and you were not going to get paid until the next week. All of a sudden, someone brought over food not only for you, but also enough for your entire family to eat. God made a way for you to eat when it seemed like there was no other alternative.

Maybe if the previous example did not pertain to you perhaps you can relate to your bills being due. All of a sudden you receive a check in the mail, someone handed you some money, or maybe you were able to shuffle your bills in order to pay them or just to buy some food. If so, you need to give God thanks right now. Do not ever be so proud that you cannot take time out to stop and thank Him.

This is all about just recognizing your miracles and knowing that you did not do them on your own. We act, sometimes, as if we made ourselves. Without a doubt God made us all. God also made each miracle that has happened in our lives. It is not what we call sometimes, "a stroke of luck." Neither is it what we may call "being in the right place at right time," or "I am just a genius."

When miracles and signs happen frequently we often get complacent and think that we have made them happen. Or else, we may think the miracles and signs that happened are common, and that is what God is supposed to do for His flocks, and that it is no big deal. We not only should just recognize our miracles, but also give God the glory for them. We must stop taking God for granted. We need to start obeying God's Commandments and Statues that were given to us by Moses. As you can see by the miracles, that, not only happened in my life but yours too, that God is still doing spectacular things and has not left us or forgotten about us. We have left God out and forgotten about Him.

Chapter 13

WINDING UP

While I am in the process of winding up things, I would like to know are you going to continue to be like the Pharisees? The reason that I had testified to you regarding these miracles was so that it would help you to know more about God and believe in Him. On top of that, you could get a glimpse of what God has done for me and for others.

In addition, these wonders should also make you look back over your life and remember what God has done for you. You can see that you have not been short changed at all. Therefore, why are you still not believing and not giving God the praise that is due to Him?

Whether you are a Pharisees, Sadducees, Democrats, or Republicans, we are all God's sheep. God made us all. You may be able to also recollect that many mystery cult religions through their research tried to get things precise in their belief in God. They were heading in the right direction, but they just kept getting on the wrong track. They could not get it right. We must keep in mind that God created them also whether it was in 4000 BC or 2017.

All of our praises should be going to the one and only one that made us, who is God. Why do we keep deviating? Just as many mystery cult religions have done before, we tend to want to follow down that same wrong track. Most often times just like with anything, we have to keep doing it until we get it right, and religion is no exception to the rule. We are all made in God's image. We are magnificently made. God gave us the power to do everything. It should not be too difficult to figure out why we are privileged to it. If you do not know, it is through Jesus Christ. It is all about the love and faith we have through Him. With that being said, yes, we can move mountains. Whether moving mountains is merely a physical or a mental concept, we have to believe. Trials and tribulations will come in our lifetime when you least expect it. We have to keep our wits and keep being strong.

I guess you may be still contemplating right now to yourself about what I stated previously and thinking that it cannot be physical. If that is your perception, you need to think again. Do you recall Moses departing the Red Sea, and was not that physical? Of course it was, with God's help. It is a good thing Moses did not think the way we do. I am so glad that Moses believed. God has given us the power. We have to remember the strength that God gives us is through Jesus Christ. Now is that not what you call being magnificently made by God, or do I have to illustrate it to you in some other ways?

As I mentioned before in a previous chapter, ask for a clearer understanding when you read the Bible verses. Jesus often talked in parables. Individuals did not understand the meaning of the parables and often asked for clarification. Likewise, as individuals, if we do not understand the meaning of Bible verses today we need to ask for clarification. To each individual the meaning of Bible verses could mean different things to different people. God intended for us to ask Him for an understanding of the Bible verses. He will inform us of which verse(s) meet our situation in life. We should just sit back and think for a moment if all situations regarding everything written in the Bible was verbatim, the Bible would be so thick and heavy that we could not carry it. Can you imagine trying to take your Bible to church? Ha! Ha!

I hope that you, as God's sheep, have received a hefty portion of nourishment from my experiences. It will help you with becoming a true believer. In exchange, you can relay these messages on to others and they too can keep sharing these experiences so that it may enlighten their lives.

Looking For a Miracle...Look Within Your Life

With many miracles deriving from each of our experiences, the message will be clearly disseminated throughout the world and everyone would become true believers. *"But ye shall receive power, after that the Holy Ghost is come upon you: and ye shall be witnesses unto me both in Jerusalem, and in all Judaea, and in Samaria, and unto the uttermost part of the earth" (Acts 1:8).* The bottom line is that we are all witnesses whether we want to testify or not.

I know for myself that God is real. These miracles I have shared have assisted me in illustrating to you that God is the truth. By confessing these miracles to you in this book it was a way to be able to reach more people faster and in a more distance part of the world. This is what God intended for us to do; to be a bona fide witness to everyone.

I hope as I wind things all up that you can indeed be recorded as a true believer. If you are still thinking maybe only a few miracles or perhaps no miracles have happened in your life it is because of your unbelief. Just believe, and see all the amazing things that will transpire in your life.

Tell me now are you still a doubter? Are you still looking for signs? Are you running around town waiting for some type of wonder to happen...hoping for a miracle...before you believe? If you only believe in God and do not doubt, you will see more miracles and signs happen in your life than you could ever imagine.